MAN AND MONUMENT

By FRANK FREIDEL
Professor of History, Harvard University

and

LONNELLE AIKMAN
National Geographic Senior Editorial Staff

WASHINGTON NATIONAL MONUMENT ASSOCIATION
with the cooperation of the National Geographic Society

WASHINGTON, D. C.

COVER: *Unfinished portrait of George Washington, painted from life in 1796 by Gilbert Stuart.*

FRONT ENDSHEET: *Throngs cheer Washington's victorious re-entry into New York City on November 25, 1783, in this 1850 lithograph.*

FRONTISPIECE: *Portrait of Washington, painted by Charles Willson Peale in 1779, shows him as commander in chief of the Continental Army.*

TITLE PAGE: *The Washington family coat of arms bears a 15th-century spelling in its scroll. The name probably evolved from de Wessington, which appears in earlier English records.*

Produced by the Special Publications Division of the National Geographic Society as a public service

STAFF FOR THIS BOOK

Melville Bell Grosvenor	Editor in Chief
Franc Shor	Editorial Director
Robert L. Breeden	Editor
Donald J. Crump	Assistant Editor

Text by Frank Freidel and Lonnelle Aikman

Bruce Brander, Barbara Coulter, Barbara J. Hall, Geraldine Linder, Robert C. Magis, Margaret McKelway, Mary Anne McTaggart, Charlene L. Murphy, Patricia G. Rosenborg, Margaret C. Shaw, James R. Whitney

REVISION STAFF

Philip B. Silcott, Editor; Bruce Lorich, Assistant to the Editor; Tee Loftin Snell, Research

COMMEMORATIVE *medallion celebrates laying of the cornerstone of the Washington Monument, July 4, 1848.*

The ceremony fulfilled a pledge made 65 years earlier by the Continental Congress to honor George Washington.

Reverse side of the medal shows the structure as designer Robert Mills originally conceived it—an obelisk 600 feet high, growing from a circular colonnaded base.

Foreword

OUR FIRST PRESIDENT has always been the symbol of the American republic. Just as the Washington Monument dominates the Federal City bearing his name, so George Washington, as both military commander and statesman, was the overshadowing leader and proponent of enlightened virtue among the creators of the Union. It was he who marshaled the Continental forces during the eight-year struggle for independence, and he who fostered the principles of government that took shape in the Constitution. As Chief Executive, he created a powerful Presidency limited by constitutional restraints. His careful policies guided the Nation through the perils of its early years and set it on a course toward greatness.

The ideas upon which Washington based his actions are still an inspiration to the Nation. He helped put into operation the concept, daring for that day, that a free people could successfully establish their own government, "uniting security with energy." When he first took the oath of office as President, he declared that "the preservation of the sacred fire of liberty, and the destiny of the Republican model of Government are . . . staked, on the experiment entrusted to the hands of the American people."

That experiment depended in part upon the unity of the people. In his Farewell Address, Washington set forth the characteristics that he felt must bind Americans into a nation:

"The name of AMERICAN . . . must always exalt the just pride of Patriotism, more than any appellation derived from local discriminations. With slight shades of difference, you have the same Religeon, Manners, Habits and Political Principles. You have in a common cause fought and triumphed together. The independence and liberty you possess are the work of joint councils, and joint efforts; of common dangers, sufferings and successes."

While Washington firmly believed, as he emphasized in his first Inaugural Address, that Americans were the particular beneficiaries of divine providence, he was also certain that "the propitious smiles of Heaven, can never be expected on a nation that disregards the eternal rules of order and right, which Heaven itself has ordained." For the American people, he set an example of orderliness and righteousness. In his studied analysis of national problems, he arrived at sound decisions through thorough knowledge. He also brought to these problems a conciliatory attitude, listening to the opposing views of some advisers, and accepting compromise. It was in the spirit of a great mediator and unifier that he presided over the Constitutional Convention, and, although the finished document was not entirely as he would have wished, on balance he hailed it as "a new phenomenon in the political and moral world; and an astonishing victory gained by enlightened reason over brutal force."

The spread of enlightened reason was one of the ends Washington advocated in his First Annual Address to Congress. He asked Congress to aid existing educational institutions or to establish a national university, saying that "Knowledge is in every country the surest basis of public happiness," contributing inestimably to "the security of a free constitution. . . ."

The nurture of liberty, Washington emphasized in both word and deed, depends upon a government energetic yet not tyrannical, one based on the will of an enlightened nation. He commanded the Continental Army during the American Revolution to win that liberty, and as our first President he led the American people in preserving it.

FRANK FREIDEL

CAPTURED IN LIFE — *George Washington at 53. Commissioned by the General Assembly of Virginia to prepare a statue of Washington "of the finest marble and the best workmanship," French sculptor Jean Antoine Houdon arrived at Mount Vernon in October, 1785. After making a plaster life mask, Houdon cast from it two clay busts, one of which (above) remains at Mount Vernon.*

The years had been full ones for the Virginia planter. As a young man Washington enjoyed the pleasant and sophisticated colonial atmosphere into which he was born. He had also faced the dangers of frontier life during the French and Indian War.

When at 43 he accepted command of a raw Continental Army fighting for independence, he could not have imagined the hardships he would face before victory came eight years later.

In middle age, a weary Washington sought retirement from public service at his home on the Potomac River. But his country would again call him into action. In 1789 he would take on the task of building a government. The man first in war would become first in peace.

NEARLY EVERYBODY of any official or social standing in the Nation's Capital came to the cornerstone laying for George Washington's Monument on July 4, 1848.

President James K. Polk, who chose that day to sign a proclamation announcing the triumphant conclusion of the Mexican War, was there. So was an Illinois Congressman named Abraham Lincoln, best known then as an opponent of the war.

Martha Washington's grandson, George Washington Parke Custis, attended, as did the widowed Dolley Madison, the aged Mrs. Alexander Hamilton, and scores of other notables. Thousands of plain citizens traveled from far and near to show their admiration for the hero of the Revolution.

The main address for the occasion lasted an hour and a half, and in the lofty and eloquent phrases of the time cited chapter and verse in recalling the great debt owed to George Washington by all Americans.

It was delivered by the Honorable Robert C. Winthrop of Massachusetts, Speaker of the House of Representatives and sixth lineal descendant of John Winthrop, first governor of the Massachusetts Bay Colony.

Afterward, Benjamin B. French, Grand Master of the Masonic Lodge of the District of Columbia, consecrated the cornerstone—wearing the same apron and sash which George Washington wore at the laying of the cornerstone of the U. S. Capitol only 55 years earlier.

No one could have expected on that happy and congratulatory day that 37 more years, marked by engineering, financial, and political crises—and the tragedy of the Civil War—would pass before the Nation's

Introduction

memorial dream became marble reality.

As First Vice President* of the Washington National Monument Society—the organization that initiated and supported the project until Congress took charge in its final stages—I am delighted to introduce the second edition of this book, *G. Washington, Man and Monument*.

Most Americans are already familiar with the general outlines of George Washington's biography, as summarized in the following pages. They have read or heard of young George's adventures on his home plantation, of hardships he faced along the wild and little-known colonial frontier, and of the fighting experience he gained in the French and Indian War which would prove useful in leading American troops against King George's redcoats.

We all look back with respect on Washington's undisputed integrity as President, in which office he "did the new republic a mighty service," as one historian put it, "by proving that power can ennoble as well as corrupt."

Far less well known is the story of the monument raised to George Washington in the city named in his honor. Yet the history of discarded proposals, unrealized plans, and the building of the Monument itself occupied a longer time span than Washington's own life.

The memorial to Washington was first conceived as an equestrian statue in a resolution passed by the Continental Congress in 1783. Plans for the monument eventually completed in 1884 were drawn up at a quiet

meeting of influential Capital citizens at City Hall in the fall of 1833.

Washington's old friend, Chief Justice John Marshall, was elected the Society's first president. On his death in 1835, former U. S. President James Madison accepted the post. Every American President since Andrew Jackson has so served ex officio.

It was no easy task, however, or merely honorary function that the Monument group as a whole had set itself. Selecting a suitable design for the structure, raising public funds to carry it out, obtaining memorial stones, and keeping the project alive through half a century of good and bad periods in the national life required time, effort, and patience cheerfully contributed by a succession of dedicated members.

Today, we of the Monument Society are grateful to the National Geographic Society—with which we have had long and friendly ties—for publishing the Monument's saga.

We are especially indebted to the Geographic's Editor-in-Chief Melville Bell Grosvenor, who authorized the first publication of this book in 1965.

We also wish to give credit to the Geographic's Special Publications Division, whose editorial and illustrations staffs have produced a lively and detailed text illuminated by drawings and by historic and modern photographs.

As the Nation's Bicentennial year approaches, both adults and young people may find pleasure and benefit in *G. Washington, Man and Monument,* with its reminder of the principles and ideals on which his country, and ours, was founded.

*By law, the President of the United States is the Society's President.

ALFRED M. GRUENTHER
First Vice President
Washington National Monument Society

The Life of George Washington

By FRANK FREIDEL

GEORGE WASHINGTON, as generations of school children have been taught, was the Father of his Country, and, in the words of Henry Lee, "first in war, first in peace, and first in the hearts of his countrymen." Olympian among Presidents, Washington even in his own lifetime was almost obscured as a person by the awe-inspiring legend enveloping him. But behind the legend stands an impressive human being who, foremost among the Founding Fathers, wrought a new United States and guided it through its first years.

Decades of training prepared Washington for his leadership in the Revolution and the establishment of the new Republic. Born in 1732 into a planter family in Virginia, Washington received from his parents and half brothers schooling in the morals, manners, and body of knowledge requisite for an 18th-century Virginia gentleman. His birthplace at Wakefield is commemorated with a reconstructed brick mansion on the original plantation site, now a national monument.

In his youth, Washington pursued two intertwined interests that gave direction to much of his life—military arts and western expansion. War was almost a normal condition in those days, as the rivalry between England and France erupted intermittently into lengthy conflict. Washington's half brother, Lawrence, served in an expedition against Cartagena in Colombia, one of the possessions of the French ally, Spain, and named his estate on the Potomac in honor of the commander, Adm. Edward Vernon. In time, Washington acquired the property and retained the name, Mount Vernon.

At 16 Washington helped survey Shenandoah lands for Thomas, Lord Fairfax. Thereafter he spent much of his life in the saddle, surveying or soldiering in the wilderness.

In 1753, when French soldiers trespassed on lands claimed by Virginia in the Ohio country, Governor Robert Dinwiddie sent Washington, at age 21, to warn them away. The next year, commissioned a lieutenant colonel, he fought the first skirmishes in what grew into the French and Indian War. The French defeated Washington and his force of about 300 men, and in 1755 surrounded and routed the British regulars

YOUNG WASHINGTON *holds a surveying instrument while his companion pays out chain to fix distance. At 14 Washington surveyed his neighbors' fields. At 16 he plotted Lord Fairfax's lands, sleeping under "one thread Bear blanket with double its Weight of Vermin...." His surveyor's office at his father's Ferry Farm estate near Fredericksburg, Virginia, is open to the public. Wakefield, the farm on which Washington was born, is now a national monument.*

GIANT OF HIS TIME, *Washington stood six feet two and weighed 200 pounds. Gilbert Stuart's portrait is the only object in the White House that has been there since its occupancy in 1800. Dolley Madison in 1814 delayed her flight from the invading British until she safeguarded the canvas.*

MYTH GILDS THE BOYHOOD YEARS *of America's first citizen.
The famous cherry tree legend (illustrated above) depicts
a repentant George freely admitting he tried to cut down his
father's favorite tree. But the story first appeared in 1806
—seven years after Washington's death—in a biography
of Washington written by clergyman and bookseller Mason
Locke Weems.*

*Wakefield (right), his modest birthplace overlooking
Popes Creek in Westmoreland County, Virginia, vanished
in 1779. The plantation endures as a national monument,
but the house now occupying the site is a copy of a farm
dwelling of the period, as is the homestead seen in this
artist's conception.*

*But other stories from the early life of George Washington
have roots in fact. In a scene (below), keen disappointment
clouds the boy's face as he yields to his mother's pleas and
gives up hope of pursuing a career in the navy. His younger
brothers and sister witness the episode.*

MAKESHIFT RAFT,
*fashioned with "one
poor Hatchet," carries
George and his guide,
Christopher Gist,
into the wintry Allegheny
River. In 1753, Wash-
ington volunteered for
an official mission to
French Fort LeBoeuf in
Ohio country. His duty:
to warn the French to
get off the British-
claimed land; to recon-
noiter the fort's military
situation; and to win to
Britain any Indians
encountered. Here, on
the return journey, ice
floes endanger the
travelers, who shortly
had to "quit our Raft"
and swim to an island.*

under Gen. Edward Braddock. Washington, an aide to Braddock, escaped injury, although four bullets ripped his coat and two horses were shot from under him.

For several years thereafter, as a colonel commanding a force of only 300 Virginians, he undertook the difficult task of defending a 350-mile frontier against Indian raids.

From 1759 to the outbreak of the American Revolution, Washington enjoyed a placid life, managing his lands around Mount Vernon and serving in the Virginia House of Burgesses. Married to a widow, Martha Dandridge Custis, he devoted himself to a busy but happy round of life.

Like his fellow planters, Washington felt himself exploited by British merchants and hampered by British Government regulations. His experiences both as a planter and as a military leader made him increasingly dissatisfied with the Crown.

As the quarrel with the mother country grew increasingly acute, Washington moderately but firmly voiced his resistance to British restrictions. He warned that "more blood will be spilt . . . if the ministry are determined to push matters to extremity, than history has ever yet furnished instances of in the annals of North America."

Washington was elected a delegate to the

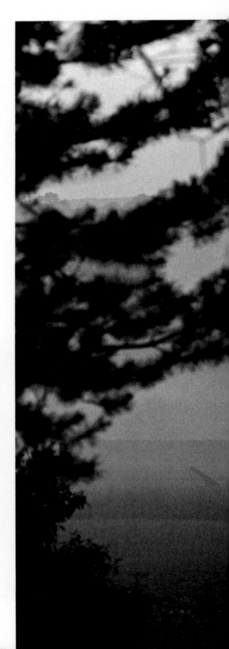

REBUILT STOCKADE *and storehouse revive Fort Necessity near Union (now Uniontown), Pennsylvania. Washington built the fort in 1754, after leading a surprise attack on a French detachment. The incident touched off the French and Indian War. A month later the French retaliated, throwing a 900-man force against the fort. After a day's fighting in a driving rainstorm, Washington surrendered and returned to Virginia with his disarmed men. The defeat—his only formal surrender—induced Great Britain to send an expedition to Virginia under Gen. Edward Braddock. Washington joined him as an aide.*

WASHINGTON READS *the burial service over General Braddock. Ignorant of frontier warfare, Braddock rejected the idea of fighting French and Indians with their own guerrilla tactics. As he advanced on Fort Duquesne (Pittsburgh) in 1755, he and half his men fell in battle. Retreating wagons ran over Braddock's grave to obliterate all signs lest Indians dig up the body for its scalp.*

Second Continental Congress. By the time it assembled in Philadelphia in May, 1775, the battles at Lexington and Concord had taken place. Now a southerner was needed to command the minutemen assembled at Cambridge. Such a leader would bring the backing of all the colonies to the struggle thus far confined to New England. Of all the delegates to the Continental Congress, Washington was most imposing in his chosen blue uniform as a Virginia militia commander, and Congress elected him commander in chief.

On July 3, 1775, at Cambridge, Massachusetts, Washington assumed command of the ill-trained army and embarked upon a war that was to last eight grueling years. The unwillingness of the British to grant concessions soon made apparent to him that this must be a war for independence—a viewpoint Congress confirmed on July 4, 1776.

Washington faced discouraging obstacles. The new state governments were usually lukewarm in their support, and Congress seldom gave him the men and supplies he needed. Washington, far from assuming dictatorial powers, was compliant with the orders of Congress, even, at times, when they went against his military judgment.

Working such long hours that biographers 13

CLYDE HARE © NATIONAL GEOGRAPHIC SOCIETY

FIRST FIRST LADY. *Martha Washington paid Charles Willson Peale $28 to paint this miniature in 1776, when she was 45. Later she described herself as an "old-fashioned Virginia house-keeper, steady as a clock, busy as a bee, and cheerful as a cricket."*

MOUNT VERNON *yearly receives more than a million visitors, who respond to Washington's own invitation: "I have no objection to any sober or orderly person's gratifying their curiosity in viewing the buildings, Gardens & ca...."*

have wondered when he found time to sleep, he somehow managed to build and maintain an army. He realized early that the best strategy for his weak, inexperienced troops was to harass the British rather than risk an all-out assault. He reported to Congress that "we should on all Occasions avoid a general Action, or put anything to the Risque, unless compelled by a necessity, into which we ought never to be drawn."

In ensuing years, from time to time he fell back slowly before superior British forces, then struck unexpectedly. It was sound strategy, and Washington an able commander.

Above all, he demonstrated his singular organizing talents and his unparalleled fortitude in the face of adversity. It was this fortitude that carried him through the bleak winter of 1777-78 at Valley Forge, its log huts now restored. It also carried him through later discouragements, even after—with the aid of French allies—he had forced in 1781 the surrender of Lord Cornwallis at Yorktown, where earthworks still bristle with cannon.

Yorktown ended the active fighting, but the Continental Army remained unpaid and restless. To Washington's acute dismay, one of the colonels proposed making him king. But, like his Roman model, Cincinnatus, he

MOUNT VERNON LADIES' ASSOCIATION (LEFT) AND THOMAS NEBBIA © N.G.S.

wished upon the conclusion of peace in 1783 to retire to his fields.

BACK at Mount Vernon, Washington came to realize that the American Nation under its Confederation Government was not functioning very well. Powers were inadequate to maintain respect for American shippers, to protect the frontier against incursions by British fur traders and Indians, or to restrain the states from engaging in economic reprisals against each other.

"Internal dissentions, and jarrings with our Neighbours," he wrote, "are not only productive of mischievous consequences, as it respects ourselves, but has a tendency to lessen our national character, and importance in the eyes of European powers."

The news that Massachusetts farmers had taken up arms against heavy taxation led Washington to lament, "We are fast verging to anarchy and confusion!" Hence he became an influential mover in the steps leading to the Constitutional Convention at Philadelphia in the summer of 1787.

Washington, presiding over the Convention, took little part in the debates, but lent his conciliatory talents and his prestige to the framing of a stronger government. When the Constitution was ratified and the new

15

CLOUDS OF CANNON SMOKE *boil above the Princeton battlefield as Washington,
on horseback with sword extended, directs artillery. Continental victory on
January 3, 1777, climaxed a daring drive that gained for Washington a military
reputation at home and abroad. Ten days earlier, on Christmas night, the general
had ferried his weather-beaten troops across the ice-clogged Delaware (left) and
staged a surprise attack on Trenton, routing the holiday-happy enemy in a two-
hour engagement.*

*Surging on toward Princeton, the Continentals encountered Trenton-bound
British reinforcements dispatched by Cornwallis to "bag the fox" beside the
now impassable Delaware. In the bleak orchard (above) outside the college town,
Washington's tired forces dealt the enemy a second stinging blow.*

*Deaf-mute William Mercer painted the action in which his father, American
Brig. Gen. Hugh Mercer, lost his life. The Historical Society of Pennsylvania
owns the primitive work of art.*

SILVER EAGLE *adorned a cockade on Washington's hat. The accessories below served the Father of his Country through the years of the Revolution. Mount Vernon displays the mementos.*

BONE-INLAID KNIFE *and fork went with the general on his campaigns.*

SILVER SPURS *were given by Washington to Lt. Thomas Lamb during cold and hungry days at Valley Forge.*

IN WHIPPING WINDS AND DRIFTING SNOW, *Washington and young Lafayette share their soldiers' hardships in the bitter winter of 1777-78 at Valley Forge. Only the general's indomitable will held together the Continental Army of 11,000 men.*

LORD CORNWALLIS'S *army marches out of Yorktown in surrender on October 19, 1781—decisive battle of the Revolution. Victory marked the end of six years in which Washington had fought the British. Declining salary, he paid his own expenses; Congress reimbursed him after the war.*

In John Trumbull's oil painting, displayed in the U. S. Capitol, Washington sits on a brown charger. His deputy, Maj. Gen. Benjamin Lincoln, on the white horse, conducts the British troops to stack their arms. Washington delegated the honor because Lord Cornwallis refused to appear.

machinery of government began to operate, the electoral college unanimously cast its ballots for Washington for President. With considerable misgivings, he accepted.

On April 30, 1789, Washington, standing on the balcony of Federal Hall on Wall Street in New York, took his oath of office as the first President of the United States (page 25). When he entered the Senate Chamber to deliver his Inaugural Address before the assembled Congress, his face was grave, his words almost inaudible.

The challenge facing President Washington and the fledgling Government gave him full reason to be grave. The United States was a weak agricultural republic in a world dominated by large, unfriendly monarchies. Its population in 1790 was only 4,000,000, of whom 700,000 were slaves; its treasury was empty; it had no army or navy worthy of the name. The Constitution was no more than a framework, silent on many details.

"As the first of every thing, *in our situa-tion* will serve to establish a Precedent," Washington wrote James Madison, "it is devoutly wished on my part, that these precedents may be fixed on true principles."

"Washington's Presidency was nothing if not painfully constitutional," Clinton Rossiter has written; Washington "did the new republic a mighty service by proving that power can ennoble as well as corrupt. . . ."

Washington was of no disposition to infringe upon the policy-making powers that he felt the Constitution bestowed upon the Congress, and, except for exploring questions of constitutionality, did not question measures it enacted. On the other hand, the determination of foreign policy became preponderantly a Presidential concern.

When Washington, accepting literally the constitutional proviso that he should negotiate treaties with the advice and consent of the Senate, appeared with a list of queries, the Senators, jealous of their prerogatives, refused him instant answers. "This defeats every purpose of my coming here," Washington fumed. Thereafter he negotiated treaties as he judged best and sent them to the Senate to ratify or reject.

Again, while the Senate, according to the Constitution, had to give its consent to Presidential appointees, Washington insisted he could remove them without permission.

As Chief Executive, Washington gave considerable authority to his department heads, and gradually came to depend upon them for advice, at first through written opinions, then as a Cabinet. At these meetings, unlike most of his successors, he ordinarily did not set forth his own opinion, and unless the Cabinet was evenly divided followed the recommendation of its majority.

This reluctance to wield executive authority single-handedly has led many later historians to feel that Washington was eclipsed by his subordinates. It is easy to overlook the fact that Washington, while slow and deliberate, was also thorough in his analysis of problems, and that he was more balanced in judgment than his subordinates. There was never any question at the time but that Washington was President, and that national policies had to have his approval. Even Thomas Jefferson in 1796 admitted, "One man outweighs them all in influence over the people."

Jefferson spoke from firsthand knowledge, since clearly, during the years when Jefferson served as Secretary of State (and thereafter also), Washington's was the controlling voice in foreign affairs. Even before he became President, he felt strongly that it would be disastrous to become embroiled in the quarrels of the European titans. He wrote in 1788: "I hope the United States of America will be able to keep disengaged from the labyrinth of European politics and Wars.... It should be the policy of United America to administer to their wants,

"G. WASHINGTON" in the map title opposite shows the autograph of the 19-year-old surveyor. Later he added more flourishes but kept the basic signature.

VICTORIOUS AFTER LONG YEARS OF WAR, *Washington resigns command of the Continental Army to resume the life of a Virginia squire, December 23, 1783.*

WASHINGTON'S MAJOR BATTLES

1. Fort Necessity   1754
2. Fort Duquesne   1755, 1758
3. Siege of Boston   1775-76
4. Long Island   1776
5. Harlem Heights   1776
6. White Plains   1776
7. Trenton   1776
8. Princeton   1777
9. Brandywine   1777
10. Germantown   1777
11. Monmouth   1778
12. Yorktown   1781

Battleground: ✕

Crossing the Allegheny

Crossing the Delaware

Surveying the Frontier

George Washington's Compass

Touring the South

TRAVELS OF G. Washington

Lisa

━━━ 1732-1758, Surveying and the French-Indian Campaign

━━━ 1759-1774, Before the War

━━━ 1775-1783, Revolutionary War

━━━ 1784-1799, After the War

★ United States Capitals During George Washington's Lifetime

Scale of miles
0   100   200

National Geographic Map by Lisa Biganzoli and John Garst after Aaron Arrowsmith's map of 1796 © N.G.S.

SOLDIER TURNED STATESMAN, *Washington (on podium) presides at the Philadelphia Convention on May 25, 1787, despite a vow never again to leave his beloved Mount Vernon. Patriots called the meeting hoping to draw together the divergent states and to build the framework for a new national government. As presiding officer, Washington seldom lent his voice to the debates that raged through the scorching summer months, but his strength became a silent, firm guideline. At times during the proceedings it looked as though the 55 delegates could never reach any sort of meeting ground.*

On one occasion the venerable Benjamin Franklin (seated far left with cane) rose and with tremulous voice moved that they pray: "The small progress we have made after

four or five weeks' close attendance . . . is, methinks, a melancholy proof of the imperfection of human understanding. . . . How has it happened, that we have not hitherto once thought of humbly applying to the Father of Lights to illuminate our understandings?" But still the wrangling grew hotter, and even Washington's faith wavered. He wrote Hamilton in July, "they are now, if possible, in a worse train than ever; you will find but little ground on which the hope of a good establishment can be formed. In a word, I almost despair of seeing a favourable issue." But two months later, on September 12, the writing committee entered the chamber with a product molded by argument and tempered by reason—the Constitution of the United States.

23

BY JUNIUS BRUTUS STERNS, FROM VIRGINIA MUSEUM OF FINE ARTS, GIFT OF COLONEL AND MRS. EDGAR W. GARBISCH without being engaged in their quarrels."

When the French Revolution led to a major war between France and England, Jefferson, then Washington's Secretary of State, was ardently pro-French, and Alexander Hamilton, his Secretary of the Treasury, equally pro-British. Washington insisted upon a middle course. Given twenty years, he believed, America could become sufficiently powerful to "bid defiance in a just cause to any power whatever." Thanks to Washington, the United States gained those twenty years.

In one respect, Washington failed to envisage the direction the American Commonwealth would take. Like many of his contemporaries, he found political parties repugnant. He expected to be "President of all the people" and was disappointed when two parties began to develop. He tried to keep both contending leaders, Hamilton and Jefferson, within his Cabinet. But his was more nearly the Hamiltonian position. At the end of 1793 Jefferson resigned, and by 1795 Washington was appointing to office only men of known Federalist views.

In creating respect for the United States, Washington felt he must comport himself with as much formality and ceremony as though he were a republican monarch. His firm insistence upon ceremony had its advantages. When Washington visited Massa-

ENGRAVING BY J. ROGERS FROM J. McNEVIN © N.G.S.   LIBRARY OF CONGRESS

chusetts at the end of his first year in office, Governor John Hancock tried to force the President to pay the first call, and, failing, gave way. The President, it became clear, would take precedence over governors.

Wearied of politics, feeling old and tired, Washington determined to retire at the end of his second term. In September, 1796, as his political testament, he published a Farewell Address in which he urged his countrymen to form a union of hearts and minds, forswearing excessive party spirit and geographical distinctions. In foreign affairs, he warned against long-term alliances. The United States should demonstrate to Europe that "we act for *ourselves,* and not for *others.*"

Washington enjoyed less than three years of retirement at Mount Vernon, for he died of a throat infection on December 14, 1799. The four-poster in which he lay still stands in his room looking down on the Potomac.

For months the entire Nation mourned him. Orators and preachers paid flowery tribute, but said less than Abigail, the wife of President John Adams, who commented to her sister: "He never grew giddy, but ever maintained a modest diffidence of his own talents. . . . Possessed of power, possessed of an extensive influence, he never used it but for the benefit of his country. . . . If we look through the whole tenor of his life, history will not produce to us a parallel."

Within this Enclosure
Rest
the remains of
Gen. GEORGE WASHINGTON.

FREED AT LAST *of public burden, Washington returns to spend his few remaining years as squire of Mount Vernon. A family portrait (left) depicts him with his wife and her grandchildren, George Washington Parke Custis and Eleanor Parke Custis.*

Making the daily rounds of Mount Vernon (right), he appears bent and white-haired. Less than three years after retirement, on December 14, 1799, he died of a throat infection, to remain for all time "first in the hearts of his countrymen."

SIMPLE FAMILY TOMB, *requested by Washington, stands on a site he selected in a pleasantly wooded glen at Mount Vernon. Honoring his wish to lie beside Martha at the plantation, Washington's heirs denied an appeal to move his body to the Capitol.*

MOURNING A DEPARTED LEADER: *Grief-stricken citizens pay homage to a stylized tombstone bearing Washington's likeness in this engraving.*

The Monument: Tribute in Stone

By LONNELLE AIKMAN

LIKE THE PYRAMIDS of Egypt or the Eiffel Tower in Paris, the Washington National Monument in the American Capital etches against the sky a profile that is known around the world.

"An exclamation point five hundred and fifty-five feet high," a novelist once described this tribute to the soldier-statesman who was first in the hearts of his countrymen. "Mathematics in action," said an architectural historian in pointing out "the purity of its abstract form." And all can see in the starkly soaring obelisk a marble symbol of George Washington's strength and vision.

Rising in a city where great Government buildings grow horizontally instead of vertically, the Washington Monument easily dwarfs everything surrounding it.

Shimmering in the sun by day, a pillar of light by night, it reaches peak display once a year when Fourth of July fireworks trace the familiar silhouette in shooting stars and showers of pyrotechnic flowers.

Washington, D. C., is hard to imagine without "the Monument," as everybody knows it. From its opening in 1888 until 1973, more than 56 million people have

29

ridden or trudged to the top for breathtaking views of the Capital. To many a citizen, the sight of this spire stirs nostalgic memories of childhood, when climbing its 898 steps was heroic challenge, and hopping and skipping down again sheer physical delight.

Yet the creation of a fitting memorial to George Washington in the city that bears his name—and whose site he personally selected—was no small task. Indeed, the project took a full century to come to fruition, and faced so many problems that at times its supporters were all but forced to abandon it entirely.

The idea first bloomed in the earliest days of the Republic, amid widespread rejoicing over the victorious Revolution.

In August, 1783, the Continental Congress, then meeting in Princeton, resolved "(Unanimously, ten States being present) That an equestrian statue of General Washington be erected at the place where the

HALF-CLAD HERO *of marble once occupied the Capitol Rotunda and later the Capitol grounds. Public disapproval caused its removal, in 1908, to the Smithsonian Institution.*

B. ANTHONY STEWART © N.G.S

residence of Congress shall be established."

The general was highly gratified by the action, as he wrote a former comrade in arms. Such flattering testimonials of regard from his country were, "and I trust ever will be," he observed, "the most pleasing reflection of my life."

Later, after Congress had voted to build the new seat of government by the Potomac, President Washington approved the spot assigned his statue by city planner L'Enfant. It should stand on the Mall, they agreed, at an intersection of lines west and south of the future Capitol and President's House.

But the fledgling Nation had more pressing problems, and Washington himself felt that the low state of the treasury scarcely warranted such unessential expenses.

So it was not until his death in 1799 that Americans suddenly realized that they had failed to provide a monument in appreciation of the Father of their Country. As hundreds of impassioned eulogies rang out from pulpit and podium across the land, Congress passed another resolution.

The new bill was sponsored by Representative John Marshall, destined to become the pioneering Chief Justice who would establish the power of the Supreme Court.

Marshall's proposal called for a marble memorial inside the Capitol building, to which Washington's remains were to be transferred when, and if, permission could be obtained from the family. Reluctantly, Martha Washington agreed.

Eventually, after decades of Congressional debates, resolutions, and correspondence with Washington's heirs, a mausoleum was provided under the Capitol Rotunda. Congress even proposed, as Washington's birthday centennial approached in 1832, that the bodies of both George and Martha should rest there.

But the tomb was never occupied. Washington's grandnephew and Mount Vernon's owner at the time, John Augustine Washington, refused to allow the remains to be moved, citing the general's will, which had directed his burial on the Virginia estate.

Henceforth the Capitol tomb would remain a tourist curiosity, and in time the repository for the black-draped catafalque on which have rested the bodies of all the

Richmond Nov. 25th 1833

Dear Sir

I received yesterday your letter of the 22d informing me that the Washington monumental society has done me the honor to chuse me as its president. You are right in supposing that the most ardent wish of my heart is to see some lasting testimonial of the grateful affection of his country erected to the memory of her first citizen. I have always wished, and have always thought that the metropolis of the union was the fit place for this national monument. I cannot therefore refuse to take any place which the society may assign me; and though my advanced age forbids the hope of being useful, I am encouraged by the name of the first vice President to believe that in him ample compensation will be found for any defects in the President.

With great respect and esteem I am dear sir your obdt

J Marshall

SUPREME COURT OF THE UNITED STATES (LEFT), NATIONAL ARCHIVES (ABOVE), AND RARE BOOKS, LIBRARY OF CONGRESS

MEN OF ACTION: *Chief Justice John Marshall (left) and former Librarian of Congress George Watterston in 1833 organized a movement which led to the formation of the Washington National Monument Society.*

WINNING ENTRY: *The design of Robert Mills, onetime draftsman for Thomas Jefferson and eminent architect of the day, captured first place in the Monument Society's 1836 competition for a Washington memorial that would "harmoniously blend durability, simplicity, and grandeur."*

Mills had already won acclaim with his memorial to Washington commissioned by the City of Baltimore, Maryland, and completed in 1829. Appointed U.S. architect by President Jackson in 1836, he designed many public buildings, among them the U.S. Treasury, the Patent Office, and the General Post Office.

Mills's plan for the Washington Monument for the District of Columbia (opposite), as he described it, outlined a "grand circular colonnaded building... 100 feet high, from which springs an obelisk shaft... making a total elevation of 600 feet."

The columned base, its frieze studded with seals of all the states, held statues of Revolutionary leaders and frescoes and paintings of battle scenes. Its entrance served as a pedestal for a classical Washington driving a triumphal chariot.

The Monument Society never accepted the ornate base, concentrating instead on raising money to construct the obelisk. Mills estimated $1,250,000 as the cost of executing his design. But the figure was conservative; at the time of its dedication, the unadorned shaft had cost $1,187,710.

Presidents, beginning with Lincoln, who have lain in state in the Rotunda above.

The Congress of the 1830's was still bent, however, on honoring Washington at the legislative heart of the Nation. In July, 1832, it authorized the then huge sum of $5,000 for a marble statue to be executed by "a suitable artist" and displayed in the Rotunda. Horatio Greenough, an American sculptor working in Italy, won the commission.

As it turned out, Greenough's classical concept of Washington, which took the form of a 20-ton seated figure, bare-chested and loosely draped, proved almost as big a fiasco as the vacant tomb (page 30).

The public was shocked when the statue was unveiled about 1841. The dignified general appeared, it was said, as if "entering or leaving a bath." Shortly thereafter, the figure was deemed inappropriate for the Rotunda floor. Removed to the grounds, it suffered the whims of the weather until Congress finally transferred it to the exhibit halls of the Smithsonian Institution.

Meantime, a civic movement was getting under way in Washington to build the towering obelisk we see today.

The project began modestly in 1833 with a paragraph in the September 24 issue of the Capital newspaper *National Intelligencer*. It announced a meeting at City Hall of "Those gentlemen who have expressed their desire" to join a group planning a monument to George Washington's memory.

Behind the new organization, which called itself the Washington National Monument Society, stood some of the town's leading citizens. Guiding spirit was the former Librarian of Congress, George Watterston, an energetic gentleman of Scottish descent who also practiced law and politics, edited newspapers, wrote novels, guidebooks, and poetry—and fathered eight children.

George Washington's old friend, John Marshall, now 78 and full of honors, was elected the society's first president. After Marshall, the post went to former United States President James Madison, and since 1836—ex officio—to each successive President, from Andrew Jackson on.

Not only was the monument project linked from the beginning with the Nation's leaders, but during the next half century

its building progress alternately zoomed and lagged with the ups and downs in the fortunes of the country at large.

Andrew Jackson began his second term the same year the Monument Society was founded. But even as his joyful followers celebrated the triumph of the "People's President," a bitter political war over finance was brewing among Jackson, Congress, and the Government-chartered Bank of the United States, a power in its own right.

With the national economy shaken by this dispute concerning the Bank's policies, it hardly seemed an auspicious time to seek funds for an ambitious patriotic memorial.

Nevertheless, the society launched its first drive, sending notices to leading newspapers and appealing to individuals and church, business, and civic groups. All ranks of Americans were asked to contribute, with an initial limit of $1 a person.

By 1836 some $28,000 had been collected, then invested by "gentlemen of prudence and elevated moral worth," as an announcement assured contributors. True, this was merely a trifling sum compared to the estimated million-dollar cost. But it

"WINE OF JOY" consecrates the Monument's cornerstone as Grand Master Benjamin French leads Masonic rites on the afternoon of July 4, 1848. President James K. Polk and Dolley Madison (above parasol) witness the proceedings from a nearby stand. The stone, containing many tokens of the time, was laid at the northeast corner of the foundation.

MATHEW BRADY, LIBRARY OF CONGRESS

offered sufficient promise to launch a public invitation to American architects to submit competing designs for the structure.

Contest winner was the well-known architect-engineer Robert Mills (page 32), who had already designed a smaller Washington Monument in Baltimore and would soon be creating the Treasury, Patent Office, and Post Office buildings in the Capital City.

Mills's entry fitted 19th-century taste in neoclassical art to a curlicued "T." It provided for a 600-foot obelisk surrounded at the base by a circular, colonnaded Greek temple 100 feet high. Behind the columns, 30 niches stood ready to receive statues of prominent Americans. Above the central portico, a colossal toga-clad Washington drove a battle chariot drawn by Arabian steeds (page 33).

All this had to be discarded later, when the required funds—perhaps fortunately— were lacking. Only the obelisk remained. And it was 1848 before construction began, following the Government's donation of public land near the site originally selected for Washington's equestrian statue.

"Few left the city, while great multi-

THE MEMORY
—OF—
GEORGE WASHINGTON.

EVERY true lover of his country will contribute something this day, in aid of the

Great National Monument
—TO—
WASHINGTON!

Have ready your donation, however small. The Contribution Box and the Ballot Box are this day side by side at every Poll in the United States.

The County in this State making the largest contribution in proportion to the number of votes cast, will be presented with an elegant three-quarter size MARBLE STATUE OF WASHINGTON, valued at $500.

CALIFORNIA, Nov. 6, 1860.

☞ Please put up this notice in the immediate vicinity of the Polls on election day, so that every voter can be ready with his contribution.

UNSIGHTLY STUMP *stood for two decades as a mute reminder of the Nation's neglect. Political turmoil and dwindling funds halted construction in 1854.*

APPEAL FOR FUNDS: *Broadsides posted at polling places across the land reminded voters in 1860 of their obligation to their first President. This election brought Lincoln to the White House.*

CATTLE PEN *during the Civil War: Monument grounds serve Union forces as a stockyard and slaughterhouse in this contemporary print.*

NATIONAL ARCHIVES (ABOVE) AND LIBRARY OF CONGRESS

tudes rushed into it. . . . The weather was most propitious. . . . The spectacle was beautiful to behold." So reported the *National Intelligencer* after the cornerstone laying, on July 4, 1848, at the Monument grounds.

Gathered on the knoll's broad slopes were from 15 to 20 thousand people, including the military in dress uniforms, fraternal groups, Indian delegations, and the Federal Government's great and near-great (pages 34-5).

President Polk attended, "though in feeble health," as he wrote in his diary. So did a little-known Congressman named Abraham Lincoln, together with two other future Presidents, Buchanan and Johnson.

Also present were Martha Washington's grandson, George Washington Parke Custis; Mrs. Alexander Hamilton, still active at 91; and Mrs. James (the incomparable Dolley) Madison. Nor did commentators fail to mention another notable participant—a live American eagle chained to a draped arch for symbolic atmosphere. This very bird had greeted Lafayette 24 years before when nearby Alexandria welcomed the general on his return to the country he had helped free.

The Speaker of the House of Representatives, Robert C. Winthrop, gave the main address of the Monument's inauguration, an hour-and-a-half oration on "The Character of Washington." In consecrating the cornerstone, the Grand Master of the city's

POTOMAC MARSHES OF 1875 *covered future sites of the Lincoln Memorial and the Reflecting Pool. On reclaimed land four decades later, work started on the Greek temple honoring Lincoln. In this view, gardens of the Department of Agriculture pattern the Mall, and the abandoned Monument rises like a factory smokestack.*

Masonic Lodge wore the same apron and sash worn by Washington at the Capitol's stone-setting ritual of 1793.

That night, as fireworks sparkled and sputtered in honor of the occasion, the spectators had more to celebrate than they knew. For President Polk at the Executive Mansion was preparing a proclamation to announce some news. It would tell the Nation that Mexico had ratified the treaty ending the Mexican War and adding half a million square miles to the American West.

Less pleasant to recall is another Fourth of July celebration that took place at the Monument grounds two years later. On this occasion, President Zachary Taylor sat for

hours in broiling heat. Returning to the White House afterward, he became ill. In five days he was dead of what doctors diagnosed as cholera morbus; legend says his death resulted from eating quantities of iced milk and cherries.

FOR THE FIRST FEW YEARS the Monument grew like a marble beanstalk. To speed the process, the society had invited all the states and territories, patriotic citizens, and even friendly foreign countries to contribute stone blocks to embellish the interior walls. Among the first presented were stones from Maine, Delaware, and the Franklin Fire Company of Washington, D. C. Some went into place at the 30-foot landing as early as 1849.

From inscriptions carved on many of the 190 memorials that greet walkers at 10-foot intervals, you sense now the pride of a growing Nation. Kansas and Wyoming were territories when they sent offerings. On a block cut in 1852, California called herself the "Youngest Sister of the Union."

As sectional tension deepened before the Civil War, the word "Union" marked many a stone. "KNOWS NO NORTH, NO SOUTH. NOTHING BUT THE UNION," Indiana proclaimed proudly.

When you descend from landing to landing today, you come on blocks from such donors as the Cherokee Nation, the Sons of Temperance, and the "Ladies & Gentlemen of the Dramatic Profession of America."

Greece, "The Mother of Ancient Liberty," sent a white marble piece from the ruins of the Parthenon. Turkey's sultan inscribed his gift with sentiments composed by his court poet. A "Company of [Chinese] (Continued on page 44)

MIGHT-HAVE-BEEN MONUMENTS, *designed on the eve of the 100th anniversary of American Independence, reflected growing concern over the unsightly pile of stones that had marred the Mall for so long. Would-be designers, both professional and self-appointed, suggested various fates for the project.*

Some advocated tearing down the partially finished structure and beginning anew; others favored completing it to the height originally planned, but with variations; still others offered plans that would merely adorn the portion of the shaft already standing.

An anonymous Californian submitted to the American Architect *an interesting solution (opposite). A contemporary critic described the "spirited and poetic composition" as reflecting the "modern French Renaissance" and as having "affinity with some of the better Hindu pagodas." At the temple's footing, a Washington of massive proportions sat enthroned, with mounted guards at his sides and several feminine figures draped at his feet.*

In August, 1876, after the Monument Society had abandoned hope of raising funds to complete the memorial, it asked the Federal Government for help. Authorities settled on a simple obelisk of true Egyptian proportions after consulting with U. S. Minister to Italy George P. Marsh, an authority on architecture. The U. S. Army Corps of Engineers began work in 1878.

ENGLISH GOTHIC *design, offered by M. P. Hapgood of Boston, resembled a cathedral tower without a sanctuary. An angel topped the soaring pinnacles and ornamented turrets.*

ROMANESQUE *bell tower, a seven-storied arrangement by Philadelphian John Frazer, held a heroic statue of Washington on horseback in the arched niche at its base.*

DYNAMIC ENGINEER *Lt. Col. Thomas L. Casey, builder of Civil War forts, took charge of the Monument in 1878 and saw the project through.*

WORK STARTS ANEW: *Engineers excavate for new underpinning after finding that the original rubble masonry base would be inadequate to support the completed structure's weight. Digging out 70 percent of the ground under the shaft, they poured a deep concrete slab below the old foundation. They then strengthened and balanced the whole by enclosing it in a concrete skirt. Broadened base (below) awaits final reinforcement before upward growth.*

HARPER'S WEEKLY (ABOVE) AND LIBRARY OF CONGRESS

GROWTH
OF THE MONUMENT

555 FEET 5⅛ INCHES

Capstone set
December 6, 1884

1884

410 FEET

1883

340 FEET

1882

250 FEET

1881

176 FEET

1880

156 FEET

1855-58
152 FEET

"Know-Nothing" period

1848-54

ORIGINAL
FOUNDATION

ADDITION TO
FOUNDATION
1878-1880

Cornerstone laid July 4, 1848

WORK PROCEEDED *smoothly on the first 152 feet of the Monument. But in 1854 construction virtually ceased for a quarter century. In 1880, U. S. Army Engineers removed four feet of inferior masonry laid by the "Know-Nothings." Thereafter, the shaft grew on an average of 80 feet annually until completion.*

Christians" presented another, covered with Oriental characters and asking ". . . can any man, in ancient or modern times, fail to pronounce Washington peerless?"

But the most famous stone in Monument history—a marble slab from the Temple of Concord in Rome—never reached its place. The gift of Pope Pius IX, it was stolen from the grounds near dawn on March 6, 1854, when the obelisk had risen 152 feet.

"A Deed of Barbarism," a local newspaper called it in reporting how a band of masked hoodlums had overpowered the night watchman and rolled the stone in a handcart to the river's edge. There, it was assumed, the thieves either broke up their prize or rowed out into the Potomac and dumped it.

The block was never recovered, nor was anyone arrested for the crime. It was common belief, however, later substantiated by confessed participants, that the vandals were members of the American, or "Know-Nothing," Party, then campaigning against Roman Catholics and foreigners.

The following year, several of the Washington Know-Nothings seized control of the Monument Society by an illegal election. But the usurpers voluntarily returned the project to its legitimate leaders after several years, having added a few feet of inferior stonework that had to be removed.

Now the Civil War loomed. All work on the Monument ceased, despite the society's redoubled efforts to raise money by placing collection boxes in post offices and at voting polls—including those for the national election that brought Abraham Lincoln to the Presidency (page 36).

All during the war, the Monument stump stood as a reminder of the break between the states. Soldiers in blue drilled under the

COMPLETE AT LAST! *Engineers place the solid aluminum tip onto the 3,300-pound capstone on December 6, 1884. Members of the Washington Monument Society huddle on the lower platform 500 feet from the ground. Reporters and invited guests climb the frail outside ladder for a closer look under an American flag drawn erroneously by a contemporary artist. Newspapers hailed the Monument's completion, accomplished without a single loss of life.*

DEDICATION DAY: *Crowds braved cold winds that "seemed to come from every point of the compass" to witness the ceremony on February 21, 1885. Many spectators took refuge from the cold in the pavilion erected for the occasion at the Monument's base. Others watched from carriages.*

Pioneer photographer Mathew Brady took this picture of Lt. Gen. Philip H. Sheridan's troops lined up for review by President Chester A. Arthur (above).

Shortly afterward, the Chief Executive doffed his silk hat and put aside his doeskin gloves. ". . . I do now," he said, ". . . in behalf of the people, receive this Monument . . . and declare it dedicated from this time forth to the immortal name and memory of George Washington."

The procession moved on to the Capitol to hear an address prepared by Robert Winthrop, principal speaker at the 1848 cornerstone ceremony.

The newly laid-out Ellipse, a park south of the White House, spreads toward B Street, today's Constitution Avenue.

TEST BORE,
TO BEDROCK
102 FEET

LOAM, FILL,
AND CLAY

SAND, CLAY, AND GRAVEL

BLUE CLAY

BEDROCK

N

130 FEET

Plan showing location
of test bores

MONUMENT AT A GLANCE

Cornerstone laid	July 4, 1848
Dedicated	February 21, 1885
Opened to public	September 10, 1888
Total cost to dedication	$1,187,710
Material used on face of shaft	White marble*
Height from floor	555 feet 5⅛ inches
Width at base	55 feet 1½ inches
Width at top of shaft	34 feet 5½ inches
Thickness of walls at base	15 feet
Thickness of walls at top of shaft	18 inches
Weight of monument	81,120 tons
Weight of foundation	36,912 tons
Depth of foundation	36 feet 10 inches
Area of foundation	16,002 square feet
Memorial stones	190
Present elevator installed	1959
Elevator ascent/descent	70 seconds/60 seconds
Exterior cleaned and pointed	1934 and 1964

*From Maryland and Massachusetts

SPONGY SOIL *of sand and clay prevented deep terracing of Monument grounds first proposed in 1901. Lt. Col. Ulysses S. Grant 3rd directed test borings in 1930 that proved the alterations would have undermined the foundation, producing a "Leaning Tower of Washington."*

United States flag that floated over its flat top. Cattle grazed at the depot set up on the grounds to help feed the Army (page 37). Across the way, workmen raised the Capitol's new iron dome—a sign that the Union would go on, as Lincoln had said.

In the war's last days, in April, the Monument stub saw the Capitol's completed dome spangled with gas lights celebrating the fall of Richmond, then draped in black mourning for the assassinated President whose body lay in the Rotunda below.

The shaft was still untouched when Mark Twain worked as a Washington newspaperman in 1867. "It has the aspect," he wrote later, "of a factory chimney with the top broken off.... Cow-sheds about its base ... contented sheep nibbling pebbles in the desert solitudes ... tired pigs dozing in the holy calm of its protecting shadow."

By the centennial of Independence in 1876, the sorry state of Washington's memorial had needled the conscience of Capital officials. Congress passed a law, signed by President Grant, providing for Government completion and maintenance of the Monument. At the same time, the Monument Society ceded the land and shaft to the United States, while Congress in turn voted to make the organization a semiofficial advisory body—a status maintained to this day.

Army Engineers on the job soon discovered, however, that the Monument's foundation could not support its proposed height. Before building further, they removed weak sections of the original masonry foundation and strengthened, broadened, and deepened the rest by filling subterranean tunnels with poured concrete (pages 42-3). So skillful was the substitution that the en-

KITES FLYING, *children race across the Monument grounds on a breezy day in late winter. Today the gleaming white tower stands alone on a grassy knoll, but until 1964 unsightly World War II temporary office buildings spread near the memorial's base.*

CYNTHIA E. BREEDEN

HIGH-PRESSURE JET *of cold water puts final polish on the Monument's exterior walls. This steeplejack performs his duties from the "sky climber," a work basket reserved for the area above platform range.*

SPIDERLIKE MASONS *on steel threads cling to the Monument, risking updrafts that set their walkway swinging. Work in 1964 included repointing corroded mortar seams, replacing cornerstones, and cleaning with sand, brushes, and water. Eight electric platforms replaced scaffolding used for the 1934 cleaning. For this unusual Fisheye-lens shot,* **NATIONAL GEOGRAPHIC** *photographer Bruce Dale leaned from the upper platform with camera on a 4-foot pole.*

FLASHES OF FIRE *seem to ignite the Monument as lightning splits the skies above Washington. Frozen in bronze on the Virginia side of the Potomac River, United States Marines strain to plant Old Glory atop Mount Suribachi on Iwo Jima.*

THOMAS NEBBIA (LEFT) © N.G.S.; A. C. CHINN, WASHINGTON EVENING STAR

SKY-HIGH WORKMAN *checks lightning rods at the Monument's apex. In the first base-to-tip scrubbing, completed in 1935, a fearless thief scaled the scaffolding and made off with a set of the platinum-tipped conductors.*

tire structure settled only about two inches.

The memorial's dimensions were changed as a result of research by the U. S. Minister to Italy, George Marsh. A true obelisk, he reported, should have a height of about ten times its base width: hence the Monument's final summit of 555 feet, 5⅛ inches, to a base 55 feet, 1½ inches square.

At long last came the push to the top, starting with a second cornerstone laid by President Hayes in August, 1880.

In his book on the history of the Washington Monument and the men who launched it, the Society's secretary, Frederick L. Harvey, described how the selected stone was brought by elevator to the 150-foot point and raised into position by derrick.

Just before workmen completed the setting, President Hayes deposited in the prepared bed of mortar a coin on which his initials and the date were scratched. Others in the party followed with similar coins.

During the same period, when the Monument had reached about one-third of its planned height, a life net that could be moved upward as work proceeded was attached to the outer walls. It saved several workmen from falling, and the Monument was completed without serious injury.

Construction on George Washington's memorial ended when the capstone was set in place on December 6, 1884 (page 45).

Hoisted inside the structure to a height of some 500 feet, the 3,300-pound stone was drawn through a window opening to a platform, then raised to a higher scaffolding by rope and pulley.

Guests brave enough to watch the concluding ceremonies close-up stood shivering at the summit, 555 feet high, on open wood platforms while a "perfect gale was blowing," as the *Evening Star* reported.

Officiating was Col. Thomas L. Casey, of the Army Engineers, who had supervised the project since the Federal Government took it over. As a solid aluminum tip was placed at the Monument's apex, "a shout went up," the *Star* recorded, "the stars and stripes were unfurled and a salute was fired."

The aluminum tip itself was news. Weighing 100 ounces, at $1.10 an ounce, it was the largest such piece yet cast, and so unusual at the time that it had been displayed in Tiffany's New York jewelry store.

One more ritual and one more President completed the building saga in 1885.

VERONICA SMITH

CHERRY BLOSSOM *princesses await the moment of the annual festival coronation.*

Drawn by the image of the impartial and just first President, Americans have often gathered on these grounds to honor heroes, celebrate victories, and register protests.

The Monument's dedication began in a pavilion at the grounds on a cold February 21, Washington's birthday falling on Sunday (pages 46-7). President Arthur, bundled in a fur-lined overcoat, his sideburns brushed to stylish points, spoke briefly, then joined the parade to warmer quarters in the Capitol's House of Representatives.

The day's main speech was composed by the venerable Robert Winthrop, who had delivered the cornerstone address 37 years before, but who was now too ill to take part. So his Massachusetts colleague, Representative John D. Long, read it for him.

"Our matchless obelisk stands proudly before us today," Winthrop had written in his long, eloquent oration. "The storms of winter must blow and beat upon it. . . . The lightnings of Heaven may scar and blacken it. An earthquake may shake its foundations. . . . But the character which it commemorates and illustrates is secure. . . ."

Yet, for all the rejoicing, it was late in 1888 before the public could climb the stairs or ride the slow steam hoist and peer through the observation room's eight windows.

Indeed, the Washington Monument is never quite finished. An electric elevator replaced the steam lift in 1901, then gave way to improved models in 1926 and 1959. Today's elevator reaches the top in seventy seconds; on the way a recorded voice briefs riders on the story of the memorial.

The lighting system, too, has kept pace with American technological advances. Early visitors found the interior lighted by new—and frightening—electricity, powered by dynamo. You can still see notches in the walls from which the lamps hung, casting dim beams through the gloom.

While the Monument was still young, an ambitious program to beautify its grounds was proposed but fortunately not carried out. In 1901, the Senate's McMillan Commission for civic development recommended a landscaping project in line with L'Enfant's original plan for a grandly scenic Mall. The Monument area was to be cut into a series of terraced gardens, embellished with trees, fountains, and a great circular pool.

Since large-scale shifting of earth loads was involved, engineers made deep borings to test subsoil conditions. They found that the Monument itself would be endangered by the excavations, and the proposal was eventually abandoned.

A IR AGE PERILS brought the obelisk's first exterior searchlights in 1929, outlining its lofty peak. Later the red eyes of aircraft-warning signals began flashing from observation windows and, in 1958, from holes cut just above for better visibility.

Many other innovations marked the 1958-59 program. In the basement, a giant dehumidifier finally ended an old Monument phenomenon—the moisture condensation that had long precipitated indoor rain.

New floodlights of more than 92-million candlepower were installed. Enveloping the shaft, they created a sword of light, like King Arthur's Excalibur, that pierces the black vault of the Capital's night skies.

Twice a year the Monument's interior is housecleaned. And twice in its lifetime (1934 and 1964) the great marble shell has been repaired and scrubbed from base to tip.

To build and remove the surrounding scaffolding in 1934-35 took three months, longer than the renovation itself. Critics of President Franklin Roosevelt quipped that "That Man in the White House" was crating up the Monument to ship it to Hyde Park.

The latest refurbishing needed only eight platforms. Strung from the top by cables powered by electric winches, they carried workmen up and down the shaft's face, patching, cleaning, and waterproofing. To reach the windswept tip, men rode the sloping surface in individual steel-barred hoists called "sky climbers."

All during the cleanup, visitors continued to arrive at George Washington's Monument and look out on his forever changing city. More than one million came in 1972.

Before climbing was prohibited in June of 1971 because of congested steps and exhausted visitors needing rescue, walking up had increased in popularity. In 20 years, the ratio of climbers to riders had risen from one in five to one in three.

The National Park Service, which administers the Monument, has had its troubles with pranksters and publicity seekers. Several tried to walk the stairs on their hands.

Until safety glass covered the openings in 1961, thoughtless people tossed out of the 504-foot-high windows anything from fruit and pennies to rifle shells and skates. A high school football team once managed to hang out its banner, and later a Polish refugee was stopped from unfurling a black shroud protesting world Communism.

One of the few authorized stunts made headlines in January, 1885, even before the Monument's dedication, when a popular baseball star caught a ball dropped from the top. And just before the glass installations, a falling telescopic lens almost killed a guard. Barely missing his head, it broke a woman visitor's wrist.

The Monument has seen five suicides. Before 1926, when window bars were installed, three men leaped out to their

CRACKLING ROSETTES *spangle the night during the annual Fourth of July fireworks, set off by the National Park Service from the Monument grounds. The obelisk, reflecting the light of 92-million candlepower, glows throughout the year.*

DONALD J. CRUMP © NATIONAL GEOGRAPHIC SOCIETY

PLUSH PADDING *makes early visitors comfortable on the "precarious" 12-minute ride to the top by steam hoist. The first electric lift, installed in 1901, cut time to five minutes. Today's elevator (below), complete with recorded message about the Monument from the National Park Service, offers standing room only for the 70-second ascent.*

death. In 1915, and again in 1949, a woman and a man jumped down the elevator shaft.

Misery, however, is a rare visitor at this spot. The Monument—surrounded by its broad, grassy knoll—serves rather as a place of perpetual celebration and recreation.

Here, on Washington's birthday each year, various patriotic groups, including the faithful Monument Society, lay wreaths and make speeches in memory of the man who was "first in war, first in peace."

Tens of thousands of spectators gather here every Fourth of July to watch the fireworks and share in the national remembrance of that hard-won freedom of long ago.

Under summer skies at the Sylvan Theatre, audiences fill temporary chairs and spill out over the grounds to watch Shakespearean programs, Cherry Blossom Festivals, concerts, and award ceremonies.

Fittingly, on Citizenship Day in September, new Americans take the oath of allegiance and salute the 50 flags, one for each state, that ring this memorial. Here, too, come political speakers on controversial subjects, and mass demonstrations like the Prayers-for-Peace Crusade in 1961 and the Civil Rights March, 200,000 strong, in 1963.

Perhaps the strangest gathering ever seen near the Monument took place in May and June of 1968 as Resurrection City rose and fell beside the Reflecting Pool. This shantytown housed some 3,000 members of the "Poor People's" march on Washington to demand more jobs and better living.

Groups protesting the Viet Nam war also rallied on Monument and Lincoln Memorial grounds. At dawn on May 9, 1970, President Nixon paid a surprise visit to talk with student dissidents at one such conclave.

In 1973, even as Mr. Nixon celebrated his second inauguration, a crowd of some 100,000 swarmed over Monument lawns to protest continued fighting in Southeast Asia.

In fact, the great white obelisk has witnessed many an event that mirrored the Nation's concerns. One such occurrence, in the spring of 1887, saw National Guard forces from 31 states converge on the Capital to compete in drills of skill and discipline.

"A thousand tents whiten the green sward that stretches around the Washington Monument," the *Evening Star* announced. "Such

VISITORS CRANE NECKS *for a look at their lofty destination while awaiting the elevator. Until prohibited from doing so in June, 1971, more than 30 percent of visitors climbed the 898 steps to the top. They may now see the memorial stones that dot the stairwell only by walking down.*

a camp has not been seen in this country since the veterans of the civil war broke their last camp in '65. Now the soldiers of the North, the South, the East and the West assemble . . . and contend in friendly strife."

Eleven years later, Spanish-American War troops stopped to rest in this same parklike space on their way south to do battle in Cuba. And again in World Wars I and II the green slopes offered a natural assembly and parade ground that sprang to life with martial bands and marching men.

Of all the shows staged with the Monument as backdrop, one of the largest and liveliest was a bond rally held July 4, 1945, between victories in Europe and Asia. An estimated 350,000 people jammed the area to see the Cavalcade of Freedom ending the "Mighty Seventh" war loan.

Performers included jeeploads of movie and stage stars, color guards and bands of the Navy, Marines, and Army Air Forces, dozens of patriotic orders, and high-ranking civic, church, and Federal officials.

The acts ranged from songs, dancing, and fireworks to an epic drama of the war and a reading of the Declaration of Independence. Seats bought for the Cavalcade purchased more than $1,250,000 in E bonds.

Through good times and bad, the Washington Monument has stood deep-rooted in American soil and ideals.

Every President since Chester Arthur has looked from the Executive Mansion toward this symbol of responsibility towering at his back door. Grover Cleveland—harried by political and personal slander—spoke of gaining courage in its serene presence.

"From the room where I conduct my high office I hourly see the Monument," said President Hoover in addressing a Joint Session of Congress on the 200th anniversary of Washington's birth. "This shaft is a thing of the spirit. . . . There is about it a mantle of pure radiance. . . ."

On early morning walks, President Truman sometimes strolled to the base of the obelisk and chatted with guards about its history. In 1946, Mr. Truman became the only Chief Executive to go to the top while in office. Together with Secretary of the Interior Harold Ickes and the Monument Society's Ulysses S. Grant 3rd, he obtained from the high windows a perfect view of the proposed site for a new Potomac bridge and of the traffic rerouting needed to reach it.

The Monument's surroundings have vastly improved since 1900, when the Mall area was an unsightly clutter of railroad tracks, haphazard buildings, and marshes.

Massive Governmental departments and the Smithsonian Institution's complex of buildings now enclose a broad, grassy swath. Still more construction, guided by the New Mall Development Plan, is under way: a new wing to the National Gallery

GIFTS OF STONE: *190 memorial blocks from around the world, like these from Newark, N. J., Vermont, and Brazil, decorate the granite walls of the stairway. Other stones came from patriotic individuals and groups.*

of Art, the National Air and Space Museum, the Hirshhorn Museum and Sculpture Garden, and an underground Metro station, all to be ready for the bicentennial year.

The Lincoln and Jefferson Memorials, dedicated in 1922 and 1943 respectively, have added grace and meaning to nearby waterside scenes. But no Capital backdrop is more dramatic than that of the starkly rising Washington Monument and the softly rounded Jefferson Memorial glimpsed through the trees from the White House.

Many recent Presidents, mindful of the scene's symbolism, have made increasing use of this setting to greet distinguished foreign visitors and to put on official functions, from ballet and fireworks spectacles to lantern-lighted state dinners. Certainly, few could fail to see the significance of these memorials to the Father of his Country and to democracy's great advocate.

At a press conference held back in the 1920's, a reporter asked President Coolidge what he thought of the then popular vogue for debunking George Washington. Mr. Coolidge turned and gazed out his office window toward the Mall. "I see," he said dryly, "that his Monument's still there."

And so is a still greater testimonial to the man's genius. As Robert Winthrop said in his speech when the Monument was completed at long last, "The Union is itself the all-sufficient and the only sufficient monument to Washington." 61

MARBLE MOSAIC *of horse and palm, salvaged from the ancient African capital of Carthage, recalls the glory of a past civilization.*

Greece's contribution originally formed part of the Parthenon at Athens; another stone is "From the Alexandria Library in Egypt." Still others represent Siam, "Friendly Bremen," Turkey, and Wales.

Donations from foreign nations indicate a far-reaching respect for the character and achievements of America's hero.

HAND PUMPER *of 1854 at the Monument's 250-foot level reflects the pride of the Philadelphia Fire Department. The Monument Society received many stones from civic and trade groups eager to share in the Monument's building. Some of the blocks went into place as early as 1849. Five years later a stone from Pope Pius IX was stolen and never recovered.*

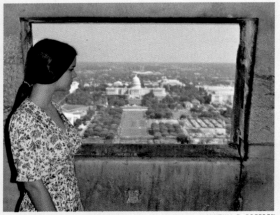

CAPITAL SKYLINE *unfolds beyond the Monument. More than a million visitors annually see this and three other Washington panoramas from the fiftieth landing.*

EAST *United States Capitol rises on its hill at the end of the Mall, L'Enfant's "Grand Avenue." Framing the proud historic dome are two Senate Office Buildings (left), Supreme Court, Library of Congress, and three House Office Buildings (right).*

The white-domed National Gallery of Art gleams to the left of the 400-foot-wide swath of green which reaches from the Capitol to the Monument grounds. Other buildings of the Smithsonian Institution, which sprang from the legacy of James Smithson, an Englishman who never crossed the Atlantic, also flank the Mall. At left center stands the Museum of Natural History. At right, the original headquarters' towers rise in red sandstone like a child's sand castle; just beyond lies the Arts and Industries Building. On the site of the parking lot, the Hirshhorn Museum and Sculpture Garden of 19th and 20th century art, and a new National Air and Space Museum—both now under construction— will open by July 4, 1976.

Sometimes called "the Nation's attic," the Smithsonian, founded in 1846, is among the world's largest museum complexes and one of America's most popular showplaces.

NORTH

Like a country manor, the White House sits in an 18-acre greensward in the heart of the city. Presidents from John Adams on have occupied this historic mansion. East and West Wings were added later to separate offices for the President and his staff from the crowded residence. The classic simplicity of the Treasury Building (right) and the ornate, rococo design of the multicolumned Executive Office Building (left) add architectural contrast to the setting.

To the north, across Pennsylvania Avenue, where Inaugural Parades pace to an end, statue-studded Lafayette Square honors Andrew Jackson and foreign military leaders—Poland's Kosciusko, Germany's Von Steuben, and France's Rochambeau and Lafayette—who helped win the Nation's fight for independence.

Rescued from demolition by President and Mrs. John F. Kennedy, handsome historic homes around the park preserve its early 19th-century dignity. The

CYNTHIA E. BREEDEN

red brick home of Commodore Stephen Decatur, completed in 1819 and now a national historic landmark, has been fully renovated. Its carriage house holds the Truxton-Decatur Naval Museum, a valuable collection of books, documents, relics, and art related to naval history. Directly across the park, Dolley Madison reigned as the city's social arbiter after the death in 1836 of her husband, President James Madison.

St. John's Episcopal Church, where many Presidents have worshiped, is hidden behind a screen of trees directly below the scalloped roof of AFL-CIO headquarters (right center). St. Matthew's Cathedral (left center), scene of the funeral of President Kennedy, lifts its green dome above a tide of business buildings that sweeps northward.

A Congressional statute prohibiting private construction above 160 feet anywhere in the city has had the effect of preserving a low skyline dominated by the Capitol and the Washington Monument.

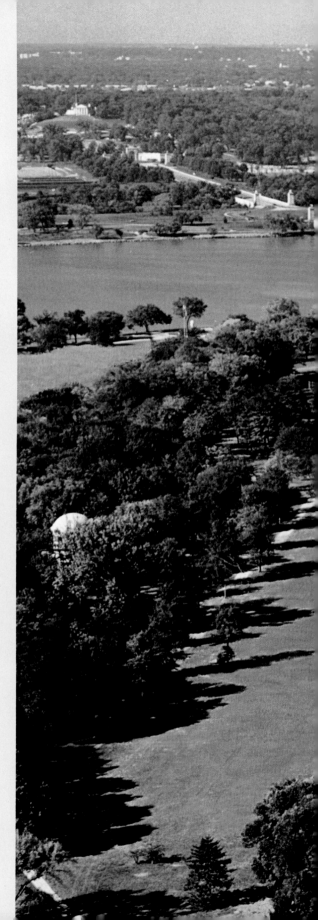

WEST

Greek temple on the Potomac, the Lincoln Memorial commands a gateway to the Nation's Capital. Like the Washington Monument, the shrine to Abraham Lincoln grew out of decades of political and financial difficulties. Dedicated in 1922 at a cost of $3,045,400, the white marble structure, with its massive Doric columns, forms a fitting frame for the giant brooding figure of Lincoln inside.

The 2,000-foot-long Reflecting Pool and a smaller Rainbow Pool, with 142 fountains, stretch almost to the Monument's base. Until the late 1960's, temporary buildings erected by the Federal Government during World War II flanked the south and north sides of the waterway, despite President Franklin Roosevelt's determination to remove them immediately after the war.

Spanning the Potomac River, the Arlington Memorial Bridge leads to the nearby Virginia shore. Beyond, the Avenue of Heroes, bearing the statue of Polar explorer Adm. Richard E. Byrd, continues to the gates of Arlington National Cemetery, where lie the Nation's honored dead. On a slope in front of the Custis-Lee Mansion (upper left), an eternal flame marks the grave of John F. Kennedy. Several hundred yards to the south, a single sentry paces in lonely cadence before the Tomb of the Unknowns.

A bridge (far right) honoring Theodore Roosevelt arches above an island named for the conservation-minded President. The island was set aside as a bird sanctuary and memorial site.

CYNTHIA E. BREEDEN

SOUTH *Amid a man-made galaxy of automobile and street lights, the Jefferson Memorial lifts its curved dome above the Tidal Basin.*

Dedicated in 1943, the 200th anniversary of his birth, the gleaming white shrine to Thomas Jefferson stands only yards from the Potomac River.

The classical structure blends architectural styles of the Pantheon in Rome with Jefferson's own designs for the rotunda at the University of Virginia and his beloved home, Monticello, near Charlottesville, Virginia.

The monument's circular interior shelters a 19-foot bronze statue of the third American

President. Engraved inside the marble dome are his ringing words: "I have sworn upon the altar of God eternal hostility against every form of tyranny over the mind of man."

Early spring transforms the Tidal Basin into a flowery fantasy; hundreds of Japanese cherry trees lining its rim unfold their pink and white petals. During summer months, foot-powered paddle boats put out from the small dock (center, left) to carry visitors over placid Potomac-fed waters.

Ribbons of light behind the memorial here mark two of the eight bridges that link the city to the Virginia shore.

69

WASHINGTON
FOR THE TOURIST

0   1/2

STATUTE MILE

Map courtesy of District of Columbia Department of Highways and Traffic